The Al-chemia
REMEDIES

Also by Leslie Zehr

The Alchemy of Dance: Sacred Dance as
a Path to the Universal Dancer

The Al-chemia REMEDIES

Vibrational Essences *from* Egyptian Flowers *and* Sacred Sites

LESLIE ZEHR

The Al-chemia Remedies
Vibrational Essences from Egyptian Flowers and Sacred Sites

iUniverse books may be ordered through booksellers or by contacting:

iUniverse
1663 Liberty Drive
Bloomington, IN 47403
www.iuniverse.com
1-800-Authors (1-800-288-4677)

ISBN: 978-1-4917-8470-9 (sc)
ISBN: 978-1-4917-8469-3 (e)

Library of Congress Control Number: 2016900393

Print information available on the last page.

iUniverse rev. date: 1/29/2016

For Lina and Abdallah
And all seekers on the path to healing.

Contents

Preface • ix

Acknowledgments • xiii

Introduction • xv

What is a Flower Remedy? • 1

      Why use water? • 5

      Why are remedies important at this time? • 6

The Al-chemia Remedies • 12

      Where were the flower remedies made? • 15

      Where were the sacred sites remedies made? • 18

      How were the remedies made? • 21

      When were the remedies made? • 23

Using the Al-chemia Remedies • 25

      Choosing a remedy • 25

      Application • 28

      Preparing a treatment bottle • 32

      Elixirs • 33

Working with Flowers • 36

      Exercise 1 - Outdoors in Nature • 39

      Exercise 2 - Cut Flowers • 39

Exercise 3 - Remedies • 40

The Remedy Profiles • 41

    The Flowers • 44

        African Daisy • 45

        Aloe • 46

        Castor Oil Plant (female) • 47

        Castor Oil Plant (male) • 49

        Easter Lily • 50

        Geranium • 52

        Indian Jasmine (common) • 53

        Indian Jasmine (red) • 54

        Jasmine • 55

        Lantana • 56

        Maleket el Leil (lunar & solar preparations) • 57

        Nile Lily • 59

        Orange Honeysuckle • 61

        Periwinkle • 62

        Powder Puff Tree • 63

        Sacred Lilac • 64

        Tamr Henna Hindi • 66

    The Sacred Sites • 67

        Dendera Temple • 68

        Temple of the Sun • 69

Glossary • 71

Bibliography • 77

Resources • 79

Preface

~~~ ~~~

My story of how this all began may not be the usual way that someone develops a new modality. I was not a flower remedies practitioner; I had not used flower remedies before I embarked on this journey. This is a story of co-creation, a calling, a gift, and an example of birthing, of moving Spirit into Matter. I was not aware of that at the time it was happening, it was only in looking back that I saw the unfolding.

My journey seems to have been a crooked road rather than a straight path. When I went to university (Virginia Tech), I went to study biochemistry. My passion was to understand how the body works but I quickly found out that this is not what you learn in biochemistry. You basically spend four years looking at the microscopic inner workings of a cell.

At the end of my studies, two weeks before graduation, I learned that my grade point average was not high enough to graduate in biochemistry. Even though I had passed all the individual courses, I would not become a biochemist. It was devastating in that moment, but it was a gift in the end. The universe *was* conspiring with me because I have neither the focus nor the passion to work in a lab.

My real interest was in body-mind work but in the 1980s in the USA, this was not an option as a university degree. For that reason, although my major was biochemistry, all my elective courses were in psychology. After not graduating in biochemistry

I took the option to change my major and stay at university one more year to graduate with a degree in psychology.

The years of studying biochemistry enabled me to understand both biology and chemistry very well. And more importantly, my studies in genetics and biochemistry provided me with an excellent understanding of how DNA works in the body. With a university background in both biochemistry and psychology, I had laid the groundwork for my own studies in body-mind therapies.

By the time my journey with the flower remedies began, I was a practicing holistic health therapist in Cairo, Egypt. I worked with many different modalities, such as aromatherapy, Reiki and hypnotherapy, all modalities that I had diplomas in but didn't feel very inspired to use.

In retrospect I see that I was studying them to prepare myself for something bigger, collecting pieces of the puzzle. I was preparing myself to receive information that would be handed down to me in the future and I needed to be able to understand it fully. I was building a base rather than a career. And being in Egypt was a huge piece of the puzzle.

One of my very first experiences when I came to Egypt in 1985 was a trip to "the island", a mango plantation about 60 kilometers south of Cairo. My first impression of it was that this must be what the Garden of Eden had looked like. After my first encounter with the island, I consequently spent fifteen summers living there among the mango trees.

My inspiration to make Egyptian flower remedies came while I was doing yet another diploma, this time in homeopathy. One of our visiting homeopaths, Ian Watson, presented a short course on the Australian Bush Flower Remedies, which I attended. After the class I spoke to Ian about my idea to make Egyptian flower remedies. He said, "Do it!" and I did it.

At the time of that course I knew very little about flower remedies. I embarked on a mission to educate myself; I spent two years studying flower remedies and researching plants in Egypt, especially plants that were traditionally used in ancient times by the pharaohs and the Prophet Muhammad. I spent a lot of time contemplating which would be the best flowers to make remedies out of.

Then in July 2000, I knew the moment had arrived; it was time to make the remedies, enough research. I had only been on the island for about a week that summer when I had great clarity. This endeavor was an intuitive process and I was being much too left-brained. I needed to trust the process and know that I would be given all the information I needed—when the time was right.

It felt as if all this time I had been "right outside the church and never thought to go in". What better place to make the remedies than right there on the island, in the Isis Garden where my children and I played? It was all right there in front of me, I just hadn't seen it. I later realized that it was not just about which flowers were used but where they were grown (on the island) and the moment in time (new millennium) that was critical to the process.

The next morning my daughter and I went into the garden and collected all the flowers that spoke to us. It was all very simple and clear, no need to think about anything. And so the remedies were birthed in that sacred garden, under the guiding light of the goddess Isis.

Acknowledgments

There were many people involved in this journey and there is much to be thankful for and to acknowledge. I am eternally grateful to the Divine for the gift of this amazing journey. I am honored.

I thank the *neter* Isis for protecting and nurturing the garden and its inhabitants until the time when these remedies could be birthed.

I thank my children for all the magical moments spent playing in that garden and to Ali for opening the door and taking me to that magical place.

To my daughter, Lina: it was a pleasure to walk this path with you. I will always cherish the experience. I am indebted to you for your assistance and the wisdom I gained from your innocence and clarity.

I would also like to thank Birgit Lindum for all her muscle testing and the work she did aligning the remedies to the meridians and elements. And to Rita Hiri for her intuiting work with the remedies in relation to the number vibrations. Both ladies added another layer to the process of how these remedies can be used.

Thank you Katarina Kratovac for editing and re-editing the manuscript. Dan Furst for his Virgo gift of seeing the smallest details that needed to be honed. Nada Jan, Antonella De Natale and Irma Zehr for showing me what was missing.

I would also like to thank Maureen St. Germain for her

generous contribution towards the publishing costs, as well as her help in the very beginning when I was transcribing the work and putting up the website. Then, as now, she gave me the support I needed to bring this project to the next level.

And last, but not least, to the flower *devas*: thank you for speaking to me and teaching me the wisdom of the plant kingdom. I am eternally grateful.

Introduction

T he Egyptian flower remedies were made in Egypt, a very
ancient land, vibrating with infinite wisdom through the
voice of our teachers, the flowers. They speak and translate into
form the vibrations and wisdom present all around us.

Flowers are the symbol of divine unfolding into manifestation.
A seed is planted and grows to its highest most perfect potential,
and then blossoms into a flower, absolute beauty—divinity in
physical form. By capturing their energy in the matrix of water,
we can use it for our own conscious evolution, to activate our
"sleeping" DNA and break old and ancient patterns. This allows
us to become whole, to unfold and blossom into our highest
potential, fully alive on every level of existence.

Over time, in our universal alchemy, we have gone through
many levels and stages, working deeper and deeper, or on a higher
and higher vibration, depending on how you perceive the levels/
stages of this process. We have explored the limits of the densest
level, the physical level, with the onset of modern medicine,
operations and drug therapy.

We have worked through the mental levels with our great
philosophers such as Plato and Descartes. We explored the
emotional realms with Freud, Jung and other great alchemists of
the mental-emotional realm. Now, in the dawning of this new
age for humanity, it is time to finish this cycle in the last phase, the
alchemy of the soul, the vibrational or energetic level, returning

us to the beginning. In order to accomplish this, we need tools that work in that realm, the vibrational realm.

The Al-chemia Remedies are a set of vibrational essences made from Egyptian flowers and two sacred sites. There are 20 remedies in this set and there will not be any more. In numerology the number 20 represents the goddess energy, creation. I only realized there were 20 remedies after making the last one. I had a sense of completion and knew they were finished. It was quite fitting as this set of remedies is devoted to the goddess Hat-hor—my mentor—my guiding light throughout my journey in Egypt.

The Al-chemia Remedies vibrate to the harmonics of the archetypal number vibrations of 1 through 10, standing as pairs or couples, twin flames. One remedy represents the number vibration in the polarity of *matter*, one in *spirit*. After ten we have completed the cycle and we begin again at a higher vibration, the ouroboros, spiraling up through infinity.

The idea to write a book about the Al-chemia Remedies came more than a decade after the remedies were birthed. I had been teaching the remedies as live classes as well as an online course. The courses were meant for people who wanted to use the remedies on themselves or to become practitioners. At the time it only seemed important to get the information to people who were already using the remedies. But then things began to shift and change.

The more I worked with the remedies via the Internet, the more I realized that it was not imperative that people actually have the physical remedy in their hands. There were many ways to access the flowers' wisdom, the remedy preparations were just one way in. I realized that the importance of my making the flower remedies was not necessarily the actual substance but the decoding of the messages—the wisdom that was held within the flowers' DNA passed down generation after generation. Making the remedy facilitated the process of doing the research. It gave us a substance, a standard to work with, apart from the flower itself.

I began to understand that through the process of potentization (shining sunlight through the auric field of the flower) we were exciting the DNA with (sun)light. When the DNA is activated its message can be read. And by putting the flowers on water we could capture its wisdom, the message it has for humanity, in the matrix of the water. The water then can be used by individuals to receive the message they need either through resonance or some modality, such as muscle testing.

The same is true for sacred sites—they have a very strong vibration that can be captured in the matrix of water. By making remedies at sacred sites we can also hold that energy in a substance that can be used in another place and time.

Science now confirms that information is held in waves. Because these messages may be produced or read through activation by light (in our case sunlight) they are commonly referred to as *light languages* by people who have the ability to intuit them.

I can easily hear the messages from flowers, I seem to "speak their language" but I am aware that many others do not—although we all have the ability to do so. So for that reason I have written their messages down, so that others can receive them as well. Flowers are full of wisdom; they have so much to teach us.

As a mentor my process is to plant seeds to give guidance, but not to ram information or my beliefs down anyone's throat. I hope that this book will inspire you to listen to the messages of flowers, use their affirmations and connect to their beauty. Nature has so much to teach us if we are just willing to listen.

I invite you to become more aware of the spaces, sacred spaces around you and connect to that energy. I hope this book will encourage others to listen to flowers and seek out their own ways to hear them speak. Information can be useful as a guide or an opening, a beginning, but experience is how we truly learn. For that reason I have included some exercises for you to try on your own so that you may hear the flowers speak.

In this book have included my own research, the messages and information I channeled when interacting to the flowers. It is original work; there is no one to reference but myself. It was when others began using and working with the remedies that I could see the effects outside of myself and my own research—that was the confirmation I needed to see the true power of these remedies.

I have included the affirmations that were given to me by the flowers as well as information received through other modalities. All of it is here, leading back to the wisdom offered to us by these particular flowers through the preparations made with them.

This book is an opportunity for me to share my knowledge and experiences with the flowers and sacred sites. It is meant as a short guide to open you to the wisdom of flowers and working with remedies—not to dictate what the *truth* is or what you should think. Find your own truth, your own message from these beautiful gifts from the Divine, these magnificent manifestations of nature.

What is a Flower Remedy?

Flower remedies are energetic preparations. They have no scent or "physical" remnants of the plant, just pure energy. Our goal in producing a flower remedy is merely to capture and preserve the energetic field of each flower in the matrix of the water. Each energetic blueprint is fixed or captured in a liquid medium, making it easily accessible for use in a variety of ways.

Oftentimes flower remedies are called flower essences but should not be confused with essential oils. Essential oils are distilled from plant material, often, but not exclusively, from flowers. Essential oils have a very strong scent and are physically/chemically active substances. Flower remedies differ from essential oils in both their composition and use.

There are many types of flower remedies, from the Bach Remedies to the Australian Bush Remedies. Although Dr. Bach, an English physician from the early 1900s, is thought of as the "father" of flower remedies, the practice of potentizing water dates back to ancient times. It was a well-known practice in both the Pharaonic and Islamic times and was probably known by all ancient cultures.

Flowers are teachers. They speak and translate into form the vibrations and wisdom present around us. Unlike *human* life forms, with over-developed minds, flowers work only for the highest good, from a place of wisdom. Flowers are the symbol of divine unfolding into manifestation.

A seed is planted and grows to its fullest and strongest potential, only then does it blossom into a flower, absolute beauty, divinity in physical form, holding the information and wisdom of the journey. By capturing this energy in the matrix of water we can use it for our own personal evolution, to assist us in our process of becoming whole, our *un-foldment*, blossom into our highest potential, fully alive on every level of existence.

Flowers are the second dimension/kingdom or second level of organization. They are meant to *attract*. They cannot move towards us so they must pull us in. This is why they are so beautiful. We notice them. We want to move closer. I also believe this is why flowers often have a fragrance, to move us closer.

We know that the sense of smell is actually a quantum sense. Scientists used to believe in the *lock and key* model of fragrance recognition. We now know that the molecules are vibrating and that the brain picks up on this vibration and that is how we recognize a fragrance. That being said, we wouldn't actually have to be able to "smell" or identify a fragrance since it is the vibration that is having an effect on us.

I have learned a lot from flowers, both as an aromatherapist and working with the Egyptian flower remedies. My understanding is that when we move in to smell a flower it has captured us in its auric field and that energy begins to work on us—whether we are conscious of it or not.

When we inhale, we are opening a pathway, an access to the brain. The olfactory system has a dangling nerve, which is actually a part of the brain. Molecules directly access the brain through the nose. Why that is important is not because of the fragrance but because we want to go deeper to access the pineal gland. The pineal gland is very sensitive to fragrance, light, sound, and waves or vibrations. People who get migraines have sensitivities in the pineal gland and this is why things such as light, smell and sound

Temple of Seti I-Abydos, Upper Egypt

can trigger a migraine. It is an over-stimulation to the system, which is already very sensitive.

Most of the orifices to access the senses are in the head. I believe that is because of the proximity to the pineal gland. It has been suggested that we don't actually see with our eyes but with our third eye. The pineal gland is so sensitive to vibration that light waves activate it and may create images. If this is true, then it is also possible that other vibrations such as sound and fragrance may be processed in or activate the pineal gland as well—just something to think about in lending more importance to *vibrationally* active substances. Descartes called the pineal gland the "seat of the soul". The importance of this highly neglected organ is only beginning to come to light.

Flower remedies are similar to homeopathic remedies in that they are energy preparations without physical properties but unlike homeopathic remedies, their energy state is not increased or *driven up*. The potency of a flower remedy is at the same energy level that was present in the original living flower. This is why flower remedies can usually be used repeatedly without a strong healing crisis or any worry of over-using them.

Flower remedies are traditionally prepared by *potentizing* water using fresh flowers and sunlight. Potentization is the transference of an energetic field to a substrate in order to make something *potent* or give it *potential* (energy). We are able to imprint the energetic field of a substance, in this case the auric field of the flower, directly into the matrix of water. This is a property that is utilized in both flower remedy and homeopathic remedy preparation.

The method of preparing flower remedies differs slightly from preparing homeopathic remedies. In the case of homeopathic remedies the water is potentized through succussion (hitting or shaking) rather than sunlight.

When preparing flower remedies fresh flowers are laid on top of a bowl of water and left in full sunlight for a period of time. The Sun shines on the flowers exciting the light in the DNA of the flowers, allowing them to "speak" their messages in light waves. The waves of light that are emitted can be imprinted or captured in the matrix of the water as the Sun shines through the auric field of the flower. For this reason, flower remedies prepared in countries with very strong sunlight such as Egypt and Australia tend to yield very potent remedies.

Why use water?

Water has the unique property of being able to shift its matrix under certain conditions. It can then hold information in its wave patterns or configuration. This is a property that has been used since ancient times but was not explained scientifically until the work of Jacques Benveniste and then later Dr. Masaru Emoto. Samuel Hahnemann, the father of homeopathy, was very much aware of this property, which is why homeopathic remedies are also made using water as the substrate.

When an energetic blueprint is transferred to the water by some force, either sunlight in the case of flower remedies, or physically (stirring or succussion) in homeopathic remedies, that blueprint is then held in the matrix of the water. This is the guiding principle behind both flower and homeopathic remedies.

In the Egyptian Pharaonic times, this was done by pouring water over a statue or a wall that was covered with hieroglyphs. Hieroglyphs are a type of writing but also contain sacred geometry, meaning that they vibrate a specific frequency. The water was potentized when it was poured over the glyphs. The water was then collected in a reservoir at the bottom of the statue or wall as in this picture from a tomb at Saqqara.

Saqqara Pyramid Complex-Giza, Egypt

The implications behind the ability of water to shift its matrix are far reaching, considering that both our bodies and the planet Earth are approximately 60%-70% water. Energy and the ability to shift and hold that energy is within us and all around us. This means that the ability to consciously shift that energy is also in our hands. A simple way to use that property to facilitate healing, the resolving of distorted energy patterns, is through the use of remedies acting on our own internal fluid matrix.

Why are remedies important at this time?

Many people talk about shifting or activating our own DNA. There is a lot to explore on this subject, as our DNA is our own personal blueprint. There is also a lot of controversy on this subject. Science has explained a lot but does not really go deeply enough into the subject to allow us to understand the magnitude of this gift.

One thing we are told is that humans presently use only a small portion of their DNA. Estimates vary from 10% to one third. Either way, there is a lot of unused DNA, ranging from 90% to two thirds. Scientists call these unused portions of DNA "junk" or "useless" DNA. The universe runs by divine order and conservation of energy, so it is very unlikely that we produce huge amounts of "useless" anything in our bodies.

There needs to be a better theory. If human scientists do not understand the subtle economies of nature it would be better for them to admit that they don't know the function of something, rather than claiming it is "junk" just because they don't understand it. As we evolve and embrace the new and ancient sciences all this begins to become clear.

One of the new theories is that this "misunderstood" DNA holds our history, the history of our ancestors, the planet and possibly the whole universe. The Mayan calendar supports this theory with its explanation of cycles and the evolution of consciousness. The calendar shows how each level is building on the level below it, making evolution an accumulation of traits and consciousness. Finally, on the seventh day (the end of the calendar) it all comes together. Humans will use everything they have, their whole brain, their history and all their abilities.

Samuel Hahnemann, the father of homeopathy, also proposed such a theory back in the late 1700s, long before science knew anything about DNA or genes. He spoke about *miasms*, inherited energy patterns that are passed down through experiences from our parents and previous generations. This is why in a homeopathic consultation a patient's family history is so important.

Hahnemann explained inheritance through a model of disease. He claimed that we pass on the energy pattern of a disease, what the parent experienced is passed on to his offspring. Hahnemann also said that something even more potent than having a disease was the fear of getting the disease. As well as proposing a theory for inheritance, he also illuminated the impact of emotional states, most importantly the devastating impact of fear on our energy system. These are influences that modern science is only beginning to understand.

This theory of inherited history and dysfunction comes up in many places, over and over again. When we stop, go inside and listen, we can feel it—we know it is true. We know that not everything we are carrying is our own personal experience. We have been analyzing, processing, detoxifying and doing shadow work—all things meant to take us deep inside so we can reach this place. All in an effort to "clean out the closets", to (en)lighten our load.

This healing work is a purification process, which allows us to shed our skin and the many skins of our ancestors that we have carried with us unconsciously for generations. But it is not an easy process, mainly because we are working in realms that are unfamiliar to us due to centuries of denial.

We cannot see what is hidden, but we can feel it. Whether we consciously know it is there or not, it sucks energy from us. Many of us are aware that we have energy leaks but have no way to identify where they are. We do hypnotherapy, past life regression and healing, all to bring to light what we cannot see but what still feeds on our energy. And because previous generations were unaware that any of this existed, they were helpless to heal it.

We, on the other hand, at this stage of our consciousness evolution, are aware enough to at least know that these energy leaks exist, even if we can't name them. For that reason we are the generations that can begin to heal these very deep issues.

Collectively we now have the ability to change. It wasn't until the 1960s that the concept of personal change became popularized. People who were born or in their teenage years at that time grew up with a different perception of life than the generations before them. This is when the "self-help" movement began. People started to understand that with some work they could change themselves. Those before them did not have this consciousness at all.

This is a huge shift because the first step in the healing process is always awakening and the belief that change can happen. Older generation have more of a strategy of coping than changing. So don't blame your parents or grandparents if they cannot change, their brains are just not formatted that way. Anyone who does transformational work knows how difficult it can be—imagine if you didn't even believe it was possible?

The good news is that because we are so deeply connected to our relatives/ancestors, when we heal the disruptions in our own energetic field, the healing moves forward and backward in time to all the future and previous generations, all of those who are connected to that vibration. Any one of us who is doing healing on ourselves will affect the whole tribe.

This is where the Al-chemia Remedies come in. They work as catalysts to activate and resolve our ancient DNA issues. These remedies were made from flowers and sites from this ancient land. They have the ability to resonate with and activate those ancient vibrations, wake up that "sleeping" DNA.

The issues we carry deep inside need to vibrate, come into the light so that we can see them and embrace them and heal them. Fear lives in the shadows because it is an illusion deep inside of us. When we bring it into the light it can no longer haunt us. It becomes *illuminated*.

There is also another aspect that is presently gaining a lot of attention as we move through this shift in consciousness. That is the fact that our history has been obscured. Mainstream archeologists rarely acknowledge "history" beyond about 6,000 years in the past. They believe that "civilization" began at that point and there is no reason to go back any further. They act as if we were unconscious beings and unaffected by anything that happened to us before we were "civilized".

This may be for many reasons. One reason may be that archeologists are just not clever enough to understand that ancient cultures, because they had very different psyches and different ways of living from ours, would be found in different places than they expected. It could also be that they need to be observed from a different perspective, such as astronomical or spiritual, as many modern independent archeologists have suggested.

It may have been a kind of "sticking their heads in the sand". They couldn't deal with what might have happened before the flood, or during the flood, so they ignored it. Possibly it was intentional. Certain groups may not want us to know what happened in pre-history. Whatever the reason for our ignorance, it is now time to deal with it and move forward.

Another theory suggests that we are not all from the same place or the same lineage. As more DNA analysis is done, this theory begins to gain strength. Whether this information has been kept from us or is just not clearly understood, it really doesn't matter. We no longer need science to tell us what does and does not exist. There are enough independent researchers presenting valuable information from a variety of sources at this time that we don't need to rely on mainstream academia funded by universities and corporations. For that reason, individuals need to take responsibility for discovering their own history, then resolving and activating it.

As we can see from the theory of miasms, our entire personal history is significant. And because the mind is very powerful, we cannot "see" what we refuse to believe exists. Our collective and personal history was repressed and thrown into the shadows.

The problem is that things in the shadows still draw energy from us whether we acknowledge them or not. These things create huge energy leaks and until we remove or heal them we will continue to be depleted on levels that we are totally unaware of. As well as energy depletions, we need to understand that there are huge energy reservoirs full of potential that lie untouched in the shadows, untapped gifts waiting to be unleashed and acknowledged.

People working in the field of metaphysics pretty much agree that in order to evolve to another dimension, frequency, density, or however one chooses to define it, we need to lighten our load, come to truth or purity. One of the factors that allow us to shift to the next level is integrity. But in order to live in integrity, we first need to know what our truth is. Otherwise, how can we step into it? Most of our beliefs come from programing either through the media or institutions such as schools. These beliefs/programming are not our *truth*. They fulfill someone else's agenda. Part of the healing process needs to be to know our true selves—on all levels.

We need to live with and engage our entire DNA to be whole. We need to evolve on all levels, live on all levels from our energy field, to atoms, to cells, to simple life forms, to our present complex beings, all at the same time. We must be able to see ourselves as part of the whole, because we are the whole. The whole universe vibrates inside of us and when we can feel and experience it, we will truly know it.

The Al-chemia Remedies

~ ~

Al-chemia Remedies are a line of remedies I created in Egypt between the years 2000-2004. The set consists of the Egyptian flower and sacred sites remedies. These remedies work as environmental essences as well as flower remedies.

Egypt is a very ancient place, vibrating with ancient frequencies. It is well known for being the land of transformation. The word Alchemy comes from the ancient Pharaonic name for Egypt: "Al-chemia", "Al-khem" or "Khemet". It means *fertile black soil* in the ancient language. It is the *prima materia* in Alchemy—the first step in the alchemic process.

Egypt is a well know power point on Earth. It is a sacred land holding its wisdom in the ancient stone structures. The temples serve as three-dimensional classrooms for the initiated. Just being here is transformative. Egypt's strong sun is very conducive for making strong remedies.

The remedies are named the Al-chemia Remedies not just because of the ancient name of Egypt (Al-khem), but also because they work as catalysts for our own personal alchemy through activating our "sleeping" DNA. We are in a period of great change, the evolution of consciousness. The Mayan calendar explains this evolution very well. It illustrates how we will be activated on all levels of existence, at the same time, after the seventh day of the Universal Cycle. This is why the calendar ended in 2011, because we will move out of space and time (see Ian Lungold's work).

Temple of the Sun and Abusir Pyramids-Giza, Egypt

The remedies were prepared during an auspicious time, the years from the new millennium leading up to the beginning of the Venus transit, 2000-2004. The last remedy was made at the Temple of the Sun while Venus was transiting between the Sun and the Earth on June 8th, 2004.

These remedies are meant to be used to assist us with the deep transformational work needed during this time, to prepare us for the next age of elevated consciousness. In order to reach this stage in our evolution, we need to lighten our load and to come to consciousness by embracing and resolving our past, both personal and collective.

The first group of remedies made was the flowers. The flowers were collected in and around the Isis garden between July 2000 and April 2001. The garden served as a temple for the flower devas.

Isis Garden and Koshk-Dabsha Island, Egypt

The second group, the two sacred sites, was created from my continuing search for the goddess. The two remedies hold the energy of the Divine Feminine, the goddess Hat-hor. The remedies are environmental. They hold space, like the womb of the goddess, holding space for our growth. They were prepared at two different sites, one in Giza and one north of Luxor.

Where were the flower remedies made?

The flower remedies were made on a very secluded island in the Nile, in a sacred garden called the Isis Garden. The island is called Dabsha Island; it is about 60 kilometers south of Cairo, in Egypt.

In esoteric practice, the Nile represents the serpent, the kundalini energy that runs through Egypt. Dabsha Island is one of the chakra points along the energy channel of the Nile River in its present location. In ancient times the Nile used to run further to the west, along the line where the pyramids now stand. This island is located half way between the points of the Dahshur and Maydoum pyramids (but due east where the river runs now).

I lived on the island every summer from 1988 to 2003. It was my *temple*, so it is fitting that I birthed the flower remedies there. I learned so much from the plants, the Bedouins that settled there and the powerful energy from the goddess Isis in the garden.

Isis Sculpture-Dabsha Island, Egypt

The Isis energy at this point was so palpable that Claudio Parmiggiani, a famous Italian artist and alchemist, built a sculpture of her in the garden in the 1980s. The sculpture is one piece of a bigger project called *Una Scultura*, which he built in four separate pieces at different locations around the world at the four cardinal points, Egypt representing the south.

The farm is a mango plantation that was started by an Englishman named Fisher in the late 1800s. According to local legend, Fisher established the mango plantation there by bringing *Alfonse* mango trees directly from India. The large *Dabsha* mango, famous in Egypt, originated on this farm and is named after the island. Fisher built himself a Tudor cottage right in the center of the island. The garden now known as the Isis Garden is just between the Tudor house (known as the *koshk* in Arabic) and "the castle".

Koshk, Isis Garden -Dabsha Island, Egypt

Fisher still haunts the *koshk*. Locals say he can be seen looking out the bay window at the front of the house. The ghost of his

Bedouin mistress has also been seen on the stairs of the house leading up to the bedrooms. There are many stories and tales about the island both from Fisher's time and more recently. It is energetically a very active place and lends itself to many unusual experiences. This is the house where I stayed when I visited the island on my first trip to Egypt in 1985.

"The castle" on the other side of the garden is a large villa that was designed by an Italian architect and built by my father-in-law, Mohamed Shaarawi. The building was never completed and is now inhabited by bats. It stands majestically overlooking the garden, giving the place an ominous or otherworldly feeling like something out of Dante's *Inferno*.

"The Castle", Isis Garden -Dabsha Island, Egypt

Until 1998, there was no electricity or clean running water on the island, just nature, no distractions. It was easy to connect with nature among the huge mango trees, which tower almost three stories high. The Isis Garden is where I used to play with my children when they were little and it was my inspiration for making the remedies. It was easy to connect to the flower devas there. It was a magical place abundant with healing energy. People who entered that garden were forever changed.

In the year 2000, I had a strong message from the Divine, that it was the time to make the flower remedies. Even though I had been studying the plants there for years, when the morning came to make the remedies, my daughter and I entered the garden and the devas made it clear which flowers would be used. That is when two years of research went out the window, in a second of awareness. The flowers had spoken.

I made flower remedies on several occasion over a two-year time period. Whenever I would hear the call, I would go to the garden and see what needed to be done. The last flower remedy was made in 2001.

Sadly, I returned to the garden for my last visit in February 2004 and was heartbroken to see the plants dead. The goddess had left the garden and moved on. It was then clear why I had gotten such a strong message to make the remedies when I did. The remedies needed to be made at that exact time because *that* energy needed to be captured; it would not remain there forever. The Al-chemia Remedies are not just a flower, or a place, but also a moment in time, an auspicious moment at the turn of this millennium. It was energy that needed to be captured and to be used elsewhere in a different place and at a different time.

Where were the sacred sites remedies made?

People who have had the opportunity to visit Egypt have benefited from the sacred energy at her sites through personal contact. Now this energy has been captured in remedies, making it available to those who have not had the opportunity to visit these sites, or those who would like to have that energy available to them outside of the site itself.

The ancient land of Egypt is an enigma. There is much mystery and speculation about who built the temples and the pyramids and why. The fact that they were built in stone is a clear sign that something needed to be preserved. The surviving monuments work as three-dimensional classrooms. Their energy and wisdom is transferred through vibration and frequency. Entering a temple is a kind of initiation.

But there is more to it than this. The temples (and pyramids) are built over much older structures. We know this from hieroglyphs found in the temple of Horus the Elder at Edfu. These places were sacred sites long before there was anything built on them. They are Earth's power points. The monuments where built in these places to mark the location and harness the energy present.

Different locations emit different types of energy. We can feel it and we can also see it by exploring what type of monument is build on that location. The more ancient the structure the purer the energy—but regardless of the structure built, we can still access the pulse from the Earth at that point. This is why we make environmental remedies. The location has a huge impact on the remedy (this is also true for the flower remedies).

The two sacred sites used to make the remedies for the Al-chemia set were chosen very unexpectedly. They are both environmental remedies that hold the energy of those sacred spaces. Both sites have great personal significance to me as they relate to the goddess Hat-hor—my mentor and guiding light.

Hat-hor is a goddess long forgotten. She reigned supreme before the patriarchy and was replaced by Isis, a less powerful goddess, in the Age of Horus. She represents one aspect of the Serpent Goddess (Divine Feminine). It is she who called me to Egypt and guided me through this process of making the Al-chemia Remedies. The flower devas are messengers of the goddess herself.

It was only fitting that the first sacred site remedy I made was made in her temple at Dendera. It was a beautiful experience to make this remedy there. It was all very spontaneous. I found myself in the temple on the roof in the chapel. The guards at the temple were very friendly; they were explaining to us how the ancients potentized Hat-hor's statue in that room. Then it hit me—I needed to make a remedy there and then to capture the energy that they used to imbue her statue with. And I just happened to have everything with me to make the remedy.

The guards made us tea and we chatted while we sat and waited for the potentizing to occur. After some time, I started to wonder how long I should leave the water to process. Suddenly I heard the call to prayer and I knew my question had been answered. It was the noon prayer, which would mean that the Sun was at its zenith. The remedy would have received the full impact of the Sun at this point. That remedy was made in May 2004.

In June 2004 I made what would be the last remedy in the Alchemia set. It was June 8th; Venus was making her transit between the Earth and the Sun, a rare and momentous occasion. A group of us decided to go out in the desert to witness Venus crossing the Sun—to celebrate the event. There was nothing to *see* because as with an eclipse, you cannot actually look at the Sun and even if you could, Venus would be too small to see.

We trekked out in to the desert in the dark because the transit would occur at sunrise and we wanted to be there. When the Sun rose and we were sitting there, not able to look at it, it occurred to me that we were all being potentized by Venus herself. As she passed in front of the Sun, the Sun shone through her auric field, imprinting itself on all bodies of water, including our own bodies. That is what we were there to do—to be touched by the goddess Venus.

As the Sun rose, I realized exactly where we were in the desert. We had gone out in the dark so my bearings were off. We were right next to the Temple of the Sun. Again, I seemed to be prepared with water and a vessel. We walked over to the altar where I prepared the last remedy—during the transit.

Hat-hor and Venus are both the archetype of the Divine Feminine. They have different names because they are from different cultures and mythologies but they vibrate the same frequency. The altar at the Temple of the Sun is an eight-pointed star—the symbol of Venus and all the Divine Feminine goddesses (Hat-hor, Ishtar, Inanna, etc.). The eight-pointed star represents the star Sirius, which is a portal to the archetypal world known to all ancient cultures. The Mayan called it the *eight-division sky place*.

There is much to say about the site but that would require a book on its own. It is sufficient to say that the altar is a portal. After making that remedy, I knew that the Al-chemia set was complete. All the remedies had been made.

How were the remedies made?

The flowers and sites for the remedies were selected by inspiration. The whole project was done through divine guidance. Each remedy has its own individual significance, as well as being part of a greater whole. Since these remedies are not just a flower, a place, but also a moment in time, their purpose is to aid us through this major period of transformation through personal alchemy.

The remedies were prepared using the same method, in the Sun, as Dr. Bach prepared his essences. The plants chosen were the ones that *called me* or that I felt pulled to make. I followed Dr. Bach's suggestion not to use crops or medicinal plants, only ornamental plants.

The ancient pharaohs used many ornamental plants. They maintained beautiful gardens, as well as using cut flowers. They used garlands of flowers when burying kings. Because their culture was well steeped in healing and esoteric wisdom, they realized the healing power of beauty and things that are esthetically pleasing.

Originally I searched for plants indigenous to Egypt, but after thinking about "what is indigenous?" I dropped that idea. Reading about the plants used by the pharaohs, I realized they had imported many plants. That was possibly 6,000 years ago. After 6,000 years it is difficult to know what is really "indigenous". Possibly everything came from somewhere else. Regions change climate and there is even speculation that we are seeded from comets and meteors from outer space. So, if it survives for thousands of years, it belongs.

From what I have seen, the energy of Egypt is so strong that things either thrive or die. If the plant survives then it belongs here (kind of like the people who come here and either grow or leave). Egypt has been invaded so many times, by so many cultures, it is truly an amalgamation of all that is. Trying to separate what is *Egyptian* from what is not is very difficult.

I had an interesting experience once with basil. I bought some purple basil seeds from the USA. They germinated and started to come up purple, and then suddenly reverted back to green like the mother plant. I felt that was nature taking over. I have no doubt that the plants that are here belong here and exist as they should.

The farm on the island is quite secluded and unspoiled. There are only a few Bedouins that have settled there. Other than that, it is pretty isolated and untouched, a sacred space. I trust that all is in divine order and that the plants that grew and were chosen were the ones that we needed to use.

Although most of the flowers were prepared by the solar method, proposed by Dr. Bach, the Egyptian flower remedies also have the distinction of having one prepared by the light of the Moon. *Maleket el Leil* is a lovely nocturnal plant. It opens and releases its fragrance from sunset to sunrise, giving the plant strong lunar qualities. Because it speaks to us at night, a Moon preparation was made capturing its energy by the light of the full moon. The lunar preparation has similar properties to the solar preparation but it is much more subtle and reflective.

There are also two preparations from the castor oil plant. The castor oil plant has two flowers—a male and a female. I was guided to make the two flowers separately. The two preparations can be used together or separately, depending on the situation. By making them separately we always have the option to use only one of them if need be.

When were the remedies made?

The flowers used to make the remedies were grown in this garden at a very auspicious moment in time at the turn of the millennium, in the nine months between July 2000–April 2001. They captured the wonderful, loving, healing Isis energy that was present during that transformational time.

At the time the flower remedies were made, the garden emanated the high priestess energy of Isis. It was a strong power point, a temple in nature. The energy in the garden has shifted and the goddess doesn't live there any more, those devas have moved on but not before giving us a gift in the form of the flower remedies. The garden became dormant just before the goddess began her trip into the underworld during the Venus transit in 2004.

Isis Sculpture-Dabsha Island, Egypt

The sacred sites remedies were both made in 2004, interestingly enough. Although the energy had shifted away from the garden and the flowers, it was still very potent at both of the site. Personally, I think it was extra potent at the sites because of the eminent Venus transit—one remedy being made just weeks before the transit and the second during the transit.

As we all know, the Earth's energy is shifting. At some point the poles will shift and I don't think anyone knows exactly what the effects of that will be. The energy in Egypt has certainly been shifting. There is a lot of darkness and heaviness moving in. I don't feel Egypt, or the sites, are as *pure* as they use to be. Or perhaps the energy at them is being used in a negative way, so it is difficult to see the light side.

Although this shift saddens me, it clarifies why the remedies needed to be made when they were—when the energy was unadulterated. This is not something that I ever could have imagined. I am grateful for trusting the guidance that was given to me to make me take action in that moment.

Using the Al-chemia Remedies

T here are infinite ways to choose and use a remedy. It is always best to use methods that you are already familiar with when choosing a remedy. Here I will mention muscle testing, pendulum, number vibration, crystals, chakras and meridians in relation to the remedies, but I will not go into an explanation of what each one is. Explaining all those modalities is beyond the scope of this book. I am making the assumption that you already know how to use these methods and if you don't, you will learn from a skilled practitioner, not from this book. For those who are not familiar with some of these modalities, I will list references and links in the resources section at the end of the book.

The Al-chemia Remedies work on deep and miasmatic issues. It is likely that you will want to use each of the remedies at some point in time. The remedies can be used individually, in combination or as elixirs blended with essential oils and floral waters.

Choosing a remedy

The best way to choose a remedy is by resonance. Resonance can be felt. To tap into this information ask: "Which remedy is calling me at this moment?" As I mentioned earlier, flowers are meant to pull us in. They cannot move toward us like power animals, so they have to inspire us to go to them to receive their message. You can easily feel this by merely tuning in or looking at pictures of the flowers. At our gatherings in Cairo, we use photographs or cards with pictures of the flowers on them. The Centre has a wall with pictures of the flowers. People just stand in front of the wall and wait for one of the flowers to call to them. Using the cards, each person lays the cards out in front of him /her and chooses one or two that really speak to him/her. If several are chosen, then we use muscle testing to eliminate or narrow down the choices. It is often the case that someone may need several remedies but not necessarily all at the same time. Muscle testing can help us to assess which is the layer that needs to be addressed in the *now*, at this particular moment, which issue needs to be dealt with first.

Often, a person needs more than one remedy, but it is always good to first check by muscle testing or pendulum. There may be several layers presenting at the same time. It is best to work one layer at a time, if possible. When muscle testing, I first find a strong muscle and then ask the client to hold the remedy bottle over their navel. I then ask the question, "is this the remedy that he/she needs right *now?*" I test the muscle again. I do this with each remedy one at a time until I find the remedy that makes the muscle lock, indicating a "yes". If I come up with more than one remedy, then so be it, if not, they are given the remedy that tested with a strong "yes". It is possible to muscle test all of the remedies but this is time consuming. It is easier to narrow them down a bit, eliminate some, and then test the others.

A pendulum can also be used in this way. I have seen this done and it works well. I do not use the pendulum myself but those that do, generally just pass the pendulum over each bottle or picture, or point to each bottle one by one until they get a strong "yes" response from the pendulum.

If you have some awareness about the issue you are dealing

with, possibly from other healing work that you are doing, you may want to use remedies that are resonating with certain chakras or meridians. The Remedy Profiles, in the second part of the book, contain information for each flower as to which chakra and meridian the remedy resonates with. Choose remedies that align with the corresponding chakra or meridian and then use attraction (pictures), muscle testing or pendulum to narrow them down and make a selection.

It is also possible to align the remedies with archetypal number vibrations. You can calculate your birth number, or cycles such as your year or month and use the remedy that resonates with the number you need at a particular moment. Rita Hiri has intuited the remedies with the Universal Vibrational Harmonics and their resonance with the numbers 1-10. Since there are 20 remedies they stand in couples, one aligned to the realm of matter, one to spirit. Any system of numerology can use the same number vibrations— use one you know to calculate what number vibration you need and use the information in the Remedy Profiles to determine which remedy that is. If your system of numerology does not separate matter from spirit, use them both together.

Once you have tuned into the Divine order, it is easy to use these correlations and apply the remedies to any modality using base 10 or base 20 systems. For example, it can be aligned with the Mayan calendar's intention for the day, which is a base 20 cycle of creation. I am not an expert on the Mayan system so I will not attempt to suggest how that might be done. It needs someone who is more knowledgeable than I am. I am just planting seeds and illustrating how these vibrations could be applied to other systems. I would also like to encourage you to apply it to other systems and feed back to me.

Birgit Lindum who teaches Touch For Health here in Cairo has muscle tested all the remedies with a surrogate to determine which meridians they resonate with. Through TFH or any other meridian-based system, once you assess which meridian needs to be balanced, you could use the corresponding remedy to work on that issue.

The remedies can also be used to program crystals. This method is useful when you want to hold a vibration. Several crystals could be programed with different remedies and used during a healing session on different parts of the body. Remedies can be chosen based on the color of the crystal or by pendulum. The information on Universal Vibrational Harmonics can help to align the geometric orientation of the crystals with the remedies.

It is also possible to choose a remedy based on the description presented. This would be the least favorable way of choosing a remedy because it goes through the logical mind. Methods that are more right-brained or intuitive tend to be more accurate. Making a choice based on the affirmations presented would be slightly more favorable as affirmations will hit us more on an emotional or feeling level than on a logical one.

Application

The Al-chemia Remedies are *not* taken internally but applied externally. There is no need to ingest a remedy. Remedies are working on the energetic level, which can be accessed in many ways, so there is no need to involve the digestive tract.

It was through the guidance given to me that I was told that these remedies should not be taken internally. After receiving that information, I then received confirmation or greater illumination from external sources. I encountered a woman who was using flower remedies and was a recovering alcoholic. She mentioned that she could not use flower remedies internally because they are preserved in alcohol. For an alcoholic even one drop of alcohol can cause an undesirable reaction.

I personally have a very strong negative reaction to alcohol; probably an allergy, and I avoid it at all costs. Given these circumstances, I feel it is an unnecessary risk, especially when we can easily absorb the remedy through our energetic body. In this book I will present many alternatives to taking them orally.

There are many ways to apply the remedies. The most powerful methods of application are in a bath, as a spray or through a navel activation. Each of these methods will be addressed separately in this section. Based on how you choose the remedy, there may be an obvious way to use it, such as in the case of crystals.

CRYSTALS

If you choose a remedy based on the crystal you intend to use it with, then the obvious way to use it would be by applying it to the crystal. The crystal should be cleansed first either in salt water or the Sun. Once it is cleansed, drops can be applied straight from the stock bottle or you can prepare a bath for the crystal with the remedy. Fill a bowl with water, add 3 drops of the remedy from the stock bottle and let the crystal sit in the bath for about 15-30 minutes. The dried crystal can be held or laid on the body as a treatment.

SPRAYS

Another way to use the remedies during a hands-on healing session is by having the practitioner apply the remedy to their hands before the session or by spraying it on the client. Alternatively, sprays can be used during hypnotherapy sessions or guided visualizations by spraying the remedy on the client before or during the session.

Sprays are also useful when using the remedies during meditation. The spray can be applied to the chakras or the entire energy body. Be sure to spray the head area to activate the third eye (with eyes closed so that you don't spray it in your eyes). Sprays can be used for creating sacred space or purifying rooms and specific areas.

The remedies can be used for rituals or ceremony. Most often the remedies are used in the form of elixirs for such events. Elixirs are a blend of remedies, floral water and essential oils. How to prepare them will be discussed at the end of this chapter.

To use the remedies as a spray follow the directions below on how to prepare a treatment bottle using a spray bottle instead of a dropper bottle.

BATH

The most common and most effective way to use the remedies is in the bath. Bathing in sacred and healing waters is a very ancient practice. In Pharaonic times this was done at both Dendera Temple and at the Temple of the Sun. Ritual bathing is a practice that should be reintegrated back into our lives, and using the remedies is a great way to begin.

Sacred Lake at Dendera Temple-Upper Egypt

To use the remedies in the bath, fill the bathtub with warm water. Create a soothing environment for healing by using candles, essential oils, and music—anything to make it more pleasant for you. You want to spend at least 20 minutes in the bath. The idea is to create an environment that is womb-like, surrounded by primordial water. You may want to repeat an affirmation, visualize or look at the picture of the flower, anything to enhance the experience.

Healing Tubs, Temple of the Sun-Giza, Egypt

Because we are doing deep healing and possibly working on miasmatic issues, it is a good idea to take ourselves back into the womb. We reconnect with that energy of birth in order to rebirth and cleanse ourselves. By adding the remedies to the bath water, and then sitting in it, you are allowing the remedy to work on the water in your own body to shift that matrix on a very deep level. Enjoy the process, be mindful and allow the healing to penetrate deeply into your energetic system.

NAVEL ACTIVATION

Another way to connect with this deep womb-like experience is through the navel (umbilicus). This is a good option if you are doing a treatment on someone else or do not have access to a bathtub. The navel is used in many Chinese and Ayurvedic treatments. All the *nadis* (energy channels in the body) end up in the navel. It is a very potent spot.

The remedies can be prepared and while the client is lying on his/her back, fill the navel with the remedy mixture. Create an environment for healing, possibly with affirmations, even some womb or navel massage. Be intuitive as how best to proceed. Using guided visualization while working with the remedies during a navel activation is very helpful.

We first activate the womb with massage and then add the remedy. The visualization takes us deep into the womb and also connects us to the *primordial mother*. Through the navel we first connect to our mother. We can then trace this connection back through our lineage; our mother, our grandmother and all the way back through space and time to the beginning of time and the primordial mother.

Preparing a treatment bottle

The Al-chemia Remedies are available as a set of stock bottles, which have been prepared from *mother tincture* to be further diluted. The stock bottles are most often used by practitioners, and then further diluted to prepare treatment bottles. If taken care of, the stock bottles can be used to prepare infinite amounts of preparations. The remedies are also available in spray bottles (treatment bottles) ready for use.

Making preparations from remedies is a *seeding* process. Think of the energy in the bottle like a match or a flame. You can light infinite candles with one match or flame. The only limiting factor is the amount of substrate/fuel (wood) present in the match, meaning the length of the match. Lighting one candle or 100 candles does not in any way diminish the flame or take away from it. This is also true of the size of the candle. Whether it is large or small candle, it only needs to ignite (seed) and it will continue burning until the wick is finished.

The same is true of remedies. You need a medium, in this case water. Whether it is small or large amount of water, it doesn't matter. Once the remedy (energy seed/blueprint) is added to the water and initiated, it will shift the matrix of all the water.

Preparing a treatment bottle is simple. It can be done in either a spray bottle or dropper bottle, depending on how you plan to use it. The amount of water added does not matter because we are not diluting the energy by adding more substrate.

Alcohol is only added to the bottle to preserve the water from going rancid. If you will be using the preparation right away there is no need to preserve the water but if it will sit and be used over time, then you will need to preserve it with alcohol or vinegar.

Use a clean amber or colored glass bottle (dropper or spray). If the remedy will be used right away or is being used in the bath it can be made in any clean container or directly in the bathtub.

Basic Treatment Bottle
Use a 30ml/1 oz. colored glass bottle (dropper or spray)
Fill 2/3 full with distilled or spring water
Add 3 drops from the stock bottle of each chosen remedy
Tap once to activate the seeding process
Top up with vodka or any type of alcohol

Elixirs

Elixirs are prepared from floral water, usually neroli or rose water, essential oils and the remedies chosen to suit the purpose or intention for which the elixir is being made. Each elixir is blended with a specific intention or focus. The elixir can be for personal use, to create sacred space or clear a space of undesirable energies. I have prepared many elixirs for different ceremonies or intentions.

The formulas came in through inspiration, either in dreams, during the dance or from traditional sources. The elixirs are used mainly for ritual or creating sacred space. To make them, I would first focus on an intention and then the process would just unfold as to which remedies and oils needed to be included.

For example, the *Lady of the Sacred Dance* was created to

provide a sacred space. I teach Sacred Dance and was doing a talk in a ballroom in a hotel here in Cairo. I knew this was not a sacred space. I also knew that people would want to experience the dance after the talk. From that inspiration, information came in as to how to create a sacred space using an elixir.

Thinking back, I had actually had a very vivid dream the night before in which I was dancing and then stopped to blend something. I didn't know at that time what the significance was but I remembered the formula very clearly (another good reason to write down your dreams). It was the first elixir I blended and used.

After the talk, people did want to experience the dance. I proceeded to spray a circle around the area we would be dancing in. It was amazing. Everyone felt the shift instantaneously. After that experience, I was fully convinced about the power of the elixirs and began blending more as gatherings and opportunities arose.

I have blended elixirs such as *Lady of the Sacred Dance* for creating a sacred space for dance and ceremony. I have also used elixirs for healing such as *Removing the Swords,* which can be used in ceremonies for closure or forgiveness.

At *The Centre for Sacred Arts in Cairo,* we had gatherings for the portal days 11:11:11 and 12:12:12, where the number vibration was the focus for blending the elixir. I blended *Unity Consciousness* for the Conscious Convergence gathering in July 2010, focusing on collective purpose and unity. More recently, my focus has been blending elixirs for the work we do in the temples in Egypt. We also do *ecstatic trance postures* (see Felicitas Goodman's work) and I have blended elixirs to enhance that experience.

Being an aromatherapist, this is my favorite way to use the remedies. If you have studied aromatherapy, then you can use essential oils to make the experience more aromatic and tap into your creativity by blending elixirs with the remedies. If you haven't, then only use oils that you are familiar with.

Elixirs are also important because when a substance has a fragrance we are more likely to inhale it. As I mentioned in the beginning of the book, we want the remedies to access the brain and the pineal gland. What better way to do that than with a wonderful elixir that is both fragrant and energetically active.

I usually dispense the elixirs in spray bottles. If you are using the elixirs in a spray bottle then be careful not to spray the elixir near the eye area as essential oils *cannot* be used in the eyes and could be harmful. Use small amounts of essential oils when blending. You will find "less is more" when working on the subtle level. They should not be over powering. It is well documented that essential oils can be more effective the less you use, so keep it to a minimum. I liken it to whispering, sometimes you can actually understand better when a person is whispering. There is a subtleness and focus and somehow it penetrates more deeply.

Generally, I use a 2-3oz (60-90ml) colored glass spray bottle to dispense the elixir. I first blend the remedies and essential oils in a small glass dropper bottle and then add this to the vinegar and floral water in the larger spray bottle.

Below is an example of one of the elixirs that I have blended. Blending for your own tastes and intentions is always more powerful because it is personal to you. Engage your creativity and inspiration and try blending your own.

Unity Consciousness
    1 drop Lantana
    1 drop Tamr Henna Hindi
    1 drop Temple of the Sun
    2 drops Petitgrain
    4 drops Frankincense
    3 drops Orange
    1 drop Bitter Orange
    1 drop Petitgrain Mandarin
    Base: 1-3 drops cider vinegar in floral water

Working with Flowers

Working with flowers or receiving messages is quite easy when you believe that you can do it. The problem is that we are indoctrinated with the belief that we cannot talk to anyone or anything but humans. Once we get ourselves out of the way it becomes simple. I am sure it is easier for some than others or that perhaps we can hear and understand the light languages from some sources better than others, but the point is to explore. You won't know until you try. And if you succeed it will open a whole new world for you. Think of it like learning another language. It is not easy at first but once you get the hang of it, you become fluent.

When I was making the flower remedies, I was given very clear guidance from the goddess as to how to do the intuiting. It all sounded very simple but I doubted my ability to do it and my worthiness to receive such important information.

I believe this is another reason I was lead to Egypt—to be isolated. At that time there was no one to teach me but the goddess herself—no one to ask, no Internet, no option to access the information except through channeling. Even books in English, and most especially on healing, were not readily available. The post is not an option if you ever wish to receive your book. So I was forced to find it within myself.

My daughter and I made the remedies together. The day we made them, I simply explained what we would be doing, what I had been *told*. She easily followed the instructions. We did not do the intuiting with the flowers at the same time we made the remedies. We went back to the garden on another day to do the intuiting.

As we entered the garden I explained to my daughter what we would be doing with the flowers this time. I told her to just sit with the plant and listen to what she had to say and take notes. She looked at me, said "OK, Mama", and walked into the garden with her pad of paper ready to receive. I just stood there with my mouth open. She had no doubt, no fear of failure, and no obstacles. She just did it. Me, I had to first break my programming in order to receive, which I did, and now it is just second nature for me to channel information. It does get easier.

Below are several suggested exercises to do with flowers. I have my Al-chemia Remedies students do these exercises with pictures of each of the flowers and then the actual remedies before they are introduced to the information that I received. It is always interesting to see how similar the information they receive is to the information I received. It is also important to see where it differs because this allows us to expand out understanding of what the flower is trying to say to us.

Everyone is a channel and women are especially receptive. So take care. Always create a sacred space for spiritual work. What is meant by a sacred space? It is a place that is free of undesirable energies—a protected space like a womb. And it is used in the same way, for growth. It allows you to be receptive without being exposed. This can be a specific place in your home or even outdoors.

There are many ways to create a sacred space. It can be done physically by having a room or area that no one else is allowed into. This makes it easy to keep the space clear. But we can also create sacred space outdoors or within other spaces. In this case it will need to be done energetically—by using an elixir, smudging or surrounding the area with white light.

In ancient Egypt they did this by drawing a circle on the ground. This defined the perimeter. A clear boundary could be set energetically by defining the space. Everything inside the circle was protected. If you are outdoors or in a space used by others, it is best to do this subtly without drawing too much attention to yourself. Drawing attention is just encouraging other people's energy to enter your space. "Where attention goes energy flows". We are trying to keep other peoples energy out, not invite it in.

Before you begin, set a clear intention about what you are doing and where you wish to receive information from. A good intention could be: "Please God/Divine/Source/Nature, allow me to hear what I need to hear at this moment, and only if it is for the highest good." As you will see from the Remedy Profiles at the back, these are messages from the light, so if you receive any harsh or disturbing information you can bet it is not the flower speaking. If so, stop the communication by saying something like "I work only with the light and I will not allow the darkness to penetrate my sacred space". Remember that you are in control at all times.

When I work with students I use my hypnotherapy background to induce them into a light trance or meditative state. They then become more receptive to the idea of listening to plants. In that case I am usually with the person either physically or by technology. If you are alone, or with others, always be aware and clear about what you are doing before entering altered states of consciousness.

Then ask the devas to speak to you. If you are outside and there are many flowers present, take note of which ones speak to you. If you are doing this with cut flowers, notice which one attracts you.

It is a good idea to have a separate journal for working with the flowers. You may want to use one with unlined paper in case you feel inspired to draw rather than write. You want to record the messages or impressions with either automatic writing or drawing. When I work with children I prefer to have them draw than to use words. Do not think about what is coming out, you don't want to get too left-brained about it—just record it and look at it later.

Exercise 1 - Outdoors in Nature

An excellent way to do the intuiting is to go into a garden surrounded by flowers and plants. Just sit, set an intention and then allow the flowers to speak to you. It can be that simple. This is a good way to begin—and may be as far as you need to go. As humanity we need to reconnect with nature, whether it is plants or animals—there is wisdom to be found everywhere. Open yourself to that connection. When doing this exercise take note of which flowers speak to you. This may change every time you repeat this exercise.

- Prepare a journal for note-taking
- Create a sacred space
- Set a clear intention
  - o "Please God/Divine/Source/Nature, allow me to hear what I need to hear at this moment, and only if it is for the highest good."
- Relax, breath, allow yourself to become receptive
- Connect to the flower by gazing intently at the one that calls you
- Silently ask the flower to speak to you
  - o "What message do you have for me?"
  - o "What is it that you would like to say?"
- Record any messages you received

Exercise 2 - Cut Flowers

The intuiting exercises can also be done with cut flowers. You can use cut flowers from the garden or ones you buy at a shop. If you receive a bouquet of flowers, notice which one is pulling you most. That in and of itself is information to take note of. Which one is calling you? If you physically have the flower in your hand you can interact with it more—smell it, or hold it to your third eye or heart chakra. Notice the different sensations you have in different places in your body. Take note of this in your journal.

- Prepare a journal for note-taking
- Create a sacred space
- Set a clear intention
  - "Please God/Divine/Source/Nature, allow me to hear what I need to hear at this moment, and only if it is for the highest good."
- Relax, breath, allow yourself to become receptive
- Connect to the flower holding it in your hand or on one of your chakras
- Silently ask the flower to speak to you
  - "What message do you have for me?"
  - "What is it that you would like to say?"
- Record any messages you received

Exercise 3 – Remedies

You can use flower remedies in a similar way to cut flowers. Hold the bottles in your hand, on different chakras, or spray it on the auric field. Notice the different sensations on different parts of the body. Be sure to take note of this in your journal.

- Prepare a journal for note-taking
- Create a sacred space
- Set a clear intention
  - "Please God/Divine/Source/Nature, allow me to hear what I need to hear at this moment, and only if it is for the highest good."
- Relax, breath, allow yourself to become receptive
- Connect to the remedy by holding the bottle in your hand or by applying or spraying it on yourself
- Silently ask the flower to speak to you
  - "What message do you have for me?"
  - "What is it that you would like to say?"
- Record any messages you received

The Remedy Profiles

The second part of this book is set up to take a closer look at each flower and sacred site individually. The pictures provided are just a thumbnail to identify the plant or site. All the remedies were made in Egypt. The flowers used were grown in and around the Isis Garden on Dabsha Island, Egypt.

The remedies are named either by the common name of the plant or the name of the site. Many of the common names are the ones the flowers gave me, which is why I tried to include the Latin name as well. The keynotes are meant to create an anchor, a focus for the remedies' use. Sometimes "less is more", a keynote allows you to focus on one piece of information and then add meaning to that as you explore the remedy and get to understand it better.

There is a description of the plant or site and the intuiting work that I did with them, explaining what each remedy is used for. This was done in several ways. The first level of intuiting was done with the actual plant or at the site. I sat with the plant in the garden and listened to what she had to say. The intuiting at the ancient sites was done over time, from several visits to the sites.

The second thing that came in, some years later, were the affirmations for the flowers. They just *downloaded* all at once as a more creative or feeling way to access the energy, giving it a destination rather than detailed description.

The rest of the intuiting was done with the remedies in meditations, activations, through sacred dance or in a bath. All of that information was compiled to create the profile.

For the flowers, I have included information on the chakras, meridians, elements and number vibrations as bullet points, in order to describe what each remedy resonates with. The energy centers are the root, sacral, solar plexus, heart, throat, third eye, crown and transpersonal point as used in traditional eastern philosophy and healing.

The information on the meridians and elements was determined through muscle testing as used in Touch For Health. The number vibrations are given as the numbers 1-9 in either matter or spirit. The two sacred sites resonate with the number 10 in both matter and spirit.

Although a lot of this information was decoded through Touch For Health and Universal Number Vibrations, it is in no way limited to those two modalities. The information can be used with any other system that is based on the same type of information. For example, the information on number vibrations can be used with any system of numerology, the information on meridians and elements with any modality using meridians and elements.

The information provided is used as a guide for those people already using the Al-chemia Remedies. This information is in no way complete. It is meant to give the reader an idea of the vast ways to use these remedies. What is presented here are suggestions and modalities that I had access to—so I included them. I encourage individuals to continue to explore and decode the messages in the modalities that they are familiar with.

For those who have never experienced the Al-chemia Remedies, or use other flower remedies, I hope you will be inspired to seek out this type of information from the flowers you use. This type of information can be useful in integrating flower remedies with other modalities as well as accessing greater understanding of the vast information encoded in their messages. I liken the different modalities to speaking different languages. Use the language that speaks to you most, whether that is numerology, energy centers, meridians or the elements.

I believe flowers are here to give us messages, wisdom and help us to heal. Using the remedies is an easy but very powerful way to access this transformational energy. It should not be taken lightly. This is deep work. Do it responsibly, with clear intentions.

The work I did with these plants was at a specific location and a specific moment in time. I do believe that the messages of these flowers may be similar over time and space. What I understand about the particular space and time I used to make the Al-chemia Remedies is that it produced a *very* potent remedy, a powerful way to access that energy.

My hope is that you will work with these flowers, whether you have the remedies or not. If you can find live flowers, then use those. You can also invoke the energy, but please try my suggestion to experience the wisdom of these flowers. They have so much to offer us.

The Flowers

AFRICAN DAISY
Dimorphotheca pluvialis
Keynote: Letting in the light

The African Daisy is a white flower with a deep purple center. It looks very much like the common daisy but has a purple rather than yellow center. It is abundant in Egypt, growing almost like weeds.

The remedy brings the feeling of white light funneling in through the crown chakra. It brings in only strong white light, closing off to the darkness. In fact, the flower does actually close in the darkness, at sunset. The white petals come together to protect the purple center. This flower reminds us to consciously protect ourselves and only let in the light. It shows us how we can protect our crown by surrounding it in white light.

- **Energy Centers:** Crown and Transpersonal Point
- **Element:** Water
- **Meridian:** Kidney
- **Number Vibration:** 7 in Matter
- **Affirmation:** *I allow the Light to illuminate all parts of my life.*

ALOE
Aloe barteri
Keynote: Protection

Aloe is a succulent. Its leaves are covered with a very thick rough skin and they are filled with a gel well known for its healing properties. The plant shoots up a stalk with many small orange bell-shaped flowers.

This remedy helps to provide emotional protection. We can use it as an energetic *thick skin* to protect the deep emotions inside. It can be used in times of great sensitivity or with highly sensitive people. It helps to create boundaries for people who are too open or in situations where we do not feel safe.

I learned from one of my students that Aloe is used in parts of Latin America for this purpose, to protect. It is often hung near the front door of homes or planted in gardens around homes to protect the sacred space.

- **Energy Centers:** Root and Sacral
- **Element:** Wood
- **Meridian:** Liver
- **Number Vibration:** 4 in Matter
- **Affirmations**: *Negative energies may NOT penetrate my life.*
- *I am safe and allow only positive, affirming energies to penetrate my life.*

CASTOR OIL PLANT (female)
Ricinus communis
Keynote: Healing Sekhmet-energy

The Castor Oil Plant is a large bushy plant often thought of as a weed. It has both male and female flowers. The seeds are abundant in oil and used to make the common castor oil.

The plant, often referred to as the "Palm of Christ", is well known for its healing properties. Edgar Cayce spoke extensively about castor oil. He believed it could be used to heal almost anything and called it "the oil that heals". He also alluded to the fact that it might actually be the energy of the plant more than the oil, the physical substance itself.

This remedy is healing in a very aggressive way, the warrior. It is the last step or stage of completion, the helping hand that will assist you in the final stage of healing. Often times it is the last little bit that takes the most courage to push through. The two remedies, male and female, may be used together if healing is needed on both levels.

The female flower (red flower) is more about birthing, bringing to daylight, making it more physical, more on the manifested level. It could be used in the birthing of a project, to bring the project into manifestation. The remedy holds strong energy of the neter Sekhmet. She is the feminine archetype of the warrior, the healer, the warrior on the subtle level.

- **Energy Centers:** Root
- **Element:** Water
- **Meridian:** Kidney
- **Number Vibration:** 8 in Spirit
- **Affirmation**: *I release negative patterns and allow the new, healthy me to emerge.*

CASTOR OIL PLANT (male)
Ricinus communis
Keynote: Healing mental-level

As I explained in the previous entry the Castor Oil Plant is healing in a very aggressive way. It assists in the last stages of healing.

The male flower (yellow flower) works more on the mental level than the female flower. It is helpful in dispelling the fears that stop us from healing. Its affinity for the solar plexus gives us the needed courage to push through.

- **Energy Centers:** Solar Plexus
- **Element:** Fire
- **Meridian:** Small Intestine
- **Number Vibration:** 1 in Matter
- **Affirmation**: *I allow healing energy into my life and release the pattern of illness.*

EASTER LILY
Lilium longiflorum
Keynote: Holding space

The Easter Lily is a bulb. It has thick green foliage. Each stalk has a flower or several flowers at the end of it. The flower is a large trumpet-shaped white flower with ruffled edges. It has a very clear plant signature; it is exactly the same shape as the uterus.

The remedy prepares us for the birth of a creation. It assists us in holding space, sacred space, the womb in which to gestate a creation. It creates a nurturing environment for healing. It is the vessel, the crucible for our personal alchemy, a place where we create the new self.

Not only does the flower look like a uterus, but the fact that the root is a bulb connects us back to the primordial mother/womb deep within the Earth, full of water and emotion.

It can be used in dream work to create a safe environment to explore other dimensions. If you do a lot a of dream work, it is important to protect yourself as you are more vulnerable when asleep.

It is excellent for making elixirs to create a sacred space for sacred work. This remedy was in fact made on Coptic Easter in 2001, just by chance.

- **Energy Center:** Transpersonal Point

- **Element:** Wood
- **Meridian:** Gallbladder
- **Number Vibration:** 3 in Spirit
- **Affirmation**: *I am safe and allow my creativity to blossom in and around me.*

GERANIUM
Pelargonium graveolens
Keynote: Awakening

Geranium is a fuzzy-leafed plant. It has small purple to pink flowers in a cluster. It is the same geranium plant that is used in aromatherapy to make the essential oil, so it is very fragrant. The remedy contains only the energy of the flower, but it can be blended with the essential oil to make a lovely elixir.

This remedy is comforting, pleasant and balancing. It aids in the joy of awakening, moving towards healing, slowly, gently. It is a good place to start for people who are just beginning a healing/spiritual path. It can serve as the first step leading to a deeper place of higher spirituality.

- **Energy Center:** Crown and Heart
- **Element:** Earth
- **Meridian:** Stomach
- **Number Vibration:** 4 in Spirit
- **Affirmation**: *I open myself to the wisdom of Nature.*

INDIAN JASMINE (common)
Plumeria alba
Keynote: Release of ego

Indian Jasmine (Frangipani) is a shrub that often grows very large, like a small tree. It has beautiful white and yellow flower clusters. The individual flowers have five petals, intertwining presenting as yellow opening into white, the opening of the ego to the Divine.

Frangipani is a well-known sacred plant in many cultures. The Hawaiian *Lei* is made from these flowers and given as an offering, a welcoming gift. It is also traditionally used in the East during wedding ceremonies, perhaps because of its intoxicating, jasmine-like fragrance.

This remedy assists the ego in moving to a higher resonance, opening to the *higher self*. It brings the full cycle of basic ego-centered thinking to enlightenment, moving us into the fifth dimension, the quintessence. It is all-encompassing. The ego exploding into enlightenment, forever moving up, always up.

- **Energy Center:** Transpersonal Point and Solar Plexus
- **Element:** Metal
- **Meridian:** Large Intestine
- **Number Vibration:** 9 in Spirit
- **Affirmation**: *I release my ego to the Divine.*

INDIAN JASMINE (red)
Plumeria rubra
Keynote: Transition

R ed Indian Jasmine (Frangipani) is also a shrub. It has beautiful five-petaled pink flower clusters growing from the nexus of the leaves.

This remedy can be used for initiation, new beginnings, a kind of breaking through to a new level. It is used for new stages of growth, such as the onset of menstruation. There is just a hint of ego to push us through. It is more innocent than the white frangipani. It is for times when the individual is just beginning to feel the collective unconscious in the heart chakra, beginning to connect to the archetypal world.

It is very mild, calming and settling. It resembles the female coming of age, opening to the physical world. It signals a new beginning, becoming aware of polarity but moving out toward the *other*. Creating an easy movement from self-connection to other-connection.

- **Energy Center:** Heart
- **Element:** Fire
- **Meridian:** Triple Warmer
- **Number Vibration:** 1 in Spirit
- **Affirmation**: *I move fearlessly into the future, connecting to the Source and embracing the next stage of growth.*

JASMINE
Jasminum officinale
Keynote: Life path

Jasmine is a large bushy vine, which seems to grow wild in Egypt. It has very small five-pointed flowers. Symbolically, vines are always about our connections to others and expanding.

The five-pointed flower represents the archetypal man, or souls, like the five pointed stars that covered the ceiling in the Pharaonic temples, the souls of our ancestors.

This remedy helps us to embark on a new path, leading the way. It holds the matrix for humanity, the individual within the collective. It is ever expanding. Small and subtle, it is the individual star among many stars, full awareness of the self among the greater many. Each star is a sun in its own solar system but still part of a larger galaxy. It can aid in awakening the awareness of the individual as part of the larger collective. It may be used to integrate idealistic personal nature as it relates to the whole.

- **Energy Center:** Transpersonal Point
- **Element:** Wood
- **Meridian:** Liver
- **Number Vibration:** 5 in Matter
- **Affirmation**: *I walk my path with courage knowing everything is in Divine order.*

LANTANA
Lantana camara
Keynote: Cooperation

Lantana is a large bush with thick, fuzzy, fragrant leaves. It has brilliant orange and yellow flower clusters. Within the flower cluster, the innermost small flowers, are yellow and the outer ones are orange.

This remedy is helpful in personal relationships and in integrating groups. Its energy can bring together strong individuals in recognition of the group as a whole, aiding them in losing the sense of ego and competition for the greater good. It allows individuals to bring in their own specific skills or gifts as necessary for creating a new collective. It is useful for conferences, group projects and unity consciousness.

- **Energy Center:** Sacral and Solar Plexus
- **Element:** Earth
- **Meridian:** Spleen
- **Number Vibration:** 8 in Matter
- **Affirmation**: *In working together, with others, my talents are supported and come to fruition.*

MALEKET EL LEIL (lunar & solar preparations)
Cestrum nocturnum
Keynote: Divine Feminine

Maleket el Leil means "Queen of the Night" in Arabic. It is a large bush with dark green waxy leaves. The flowers grow in clusters of very small, white, trumpet-shaped flowers. It blooms at night, giving off a heavenly, jasmine–like fragrance.

The energy of this plant is very feminine, lunar in nature. It works to bring in pure femininity. With this remedy you can connect to the dark, mysterious, intuitive side of yourself. Women can use this remedy to get more in touch with their true essence, the Divine Feminine within. Men can use it to connect with their muse, their *anima*, the Divine Feminine flame.

This is the only remedy to have both a lunar and a solar preparation. The lunar version was prepared during a full moon, the solar during the day in sunlight. This was done because Maleket el Leil is a lunar plant and is exalted during the night. In order to access that full potential, a lunar version needed to be made.

The lunar preparation takes us into the subtle unseen realm. The solar preparation is useful in more physical manifestations of the feminine (softening, cycles).

Lunar Preparation
- **Energy Center:** Transpersonal Point

- **Element:** Water
- **Meridian:** Bladder
- **Number Vibration:** 2 in Spirit
- **Affirmations**: *I allow the feminine lunar nature to guide me.*
- *I open to my intuition, knowing that I am connected to God.*

Solar Preparation

- **Energy Center:** Transpersonal Point
- **Element:** Water
- **Meridian:** Kidney
- **Number Vibration:** 2 in Matter
- **Affirmations**: *I open myself to the Divine Feminine nature.*
- *I allow my femininity to emerge.*
- *My body is imbued with feminine energy.*

NILE LILY
Eichnornia crassipes
Keynote: Your moment to shine.

The Nile Lily is a water hyacinth. The foliage floats down the Nile in large clumps until they reach a place where there is shallow water and they can send down roots. Once they root, they send up a flower cluster with beautiful purple orchid–looking flowers. The flower is six-pointed. The petal at the very top is dark purple in the middle, and marked with a spot of yellow at the center, almost like the Hindu *bindi* that Indian women wear on their third-eye.

It was this flower that inspired me to create this line of transformational essences. It is as if she (the Nile Lily) wanted to be the precursor and herald in the Egyptian flower remedies.

This remedy is your moment to shine. Crowds and overpopulation, getting lost in the crowd, you find your connection to earth, and you have your moment to shine. We can then take that knowing, that *grounding* and move on. Once this experience occurs, we can carry with us the knowledge of the self as integral to the whole. This remedy is useful in helping individuals recognize their path, their individual assets and connecting to them, allowing their gifts to come to fruition.

- **Energy Center:** Crown and Solar Plexus
- **Element:** Metal

- **Meridian:** Large Intestine
- **Number Vibration:** 7 in Spirit
- **Affirmations**: *I am a star shining in the galaxy.*
- *I flow through life, self-contained, grounding, connecting and manifesting.*

ORANGE HONEYSUCKLE
Pyrostegia venusta
Keynote: Cutting out the dead wood

This is a woody vine with green waxy foliage, from which orange flower clusters emerge. The flowers grow as long tubes that open into a four-petaled flower. The contrast of the green foliage and orange flowers is striking. The vine grows layer over layer on itself.

This is a powerful, joyful remedy. It helps us overcome and leave behind, the old "dead wood", holding on to the joy in life. It aids communication between individuals, moving them into harmonious action. It is for leaving the past behind and starting anew with a sense of overwhelming fun.

- **Energy Center:** Sacral
- **Element:** Metal
- **Meridian:** Lung
- **Number Vibration:** 9 in Matter
- **Affirmation**: *I allow joy into my life and leave behind all that no longer serves my happiness.*

PERIWINKLE
Vinca minor
Keynote: Journeying

The Periwinkle is a small magenta to purple pinwheel-shaped flower. There are many types of periwinkle in varying sizes and colors. This one is striking because of its intense magenta color.

This remedy aids in the development of intuition and enhances shamanic journeying and meditation. It can be used for mandala work. It is expanding and contracting, expansive but ending in a point of focus in a smooth, altered state. It enhances the state of *other dimensionality.*

- **Energy Center:** Crown
- **Element:** Fire
- **Meridian:** Heart
- **Number Vibration:** 6 in Spirit
- **Affirmations**: *I open myself to the Source of creation.*
- *I open myself to Creation itself.*

POWDER PUFF TREE
Calliandra haematocephala
Keynote: Bursting into Love

The Powder Puff Tree is a small tree with pinnate compound green leaves. Along the branches are brilliant fuchsia-colored flowers, with hair like petals.

This remedy brings in an overflowing of dynamic love. It is the heart chakra bursting with fireworks. It aids in unconditional love, bringing with it the feeling of connecting with all of humanity, as if you are in love with everyone. It helps to recreate the feeling one gets of being in love and assists one in connecting and holding this feeling toward all of life.

- **Energy Center:** Heart
- **Element:** Fire
- **Meridian:** Triple Warmer
- **Number Vibration:** 6 in Matter
- **Affirmations**: *I allow myself to love and be loved.*
- *I open myself to unconditional love, knowing that we are all connected to the Source.*

SACRED LILAC
Melia azedarach
Keynote: Hearing the call

The Sacred Lilac has green foliage with pinnate compound leaves. The flowers form large cones. Each branch of the flower cone is filled with very small five-pointed white–lilac flowers in clusters. At the center of the five-pointed flower is a small dark purple protrusion.

The remedy literally breathes communication of God's love. I call it "the call to prayer". My experience with the flower is that it is not always fragrant, but actually releases its fragrance at will. It calls to people who want to hear "the Divine is with you" by showing them the miracles of nature. It is not obvious and overwhelming, instead it manifests inside, as a peaceful connection. It is the universe confirming God/the Divine is with you, expressed as a feeling of knowing rather than intellectual thought. It is a useful remedy when feeling disconnected, or in moments of despair, wondering why you are here, and for moving from space toward incarnation.

Working with the flower further, I came to realize that it is useful in connecting to the Divine when channeling is needed. If you look at the flower closely, it has a protruding purple piece.

The image I saw was of this purple protrusion connecting directly into the crown chakra with the white petals hovering above like a funnel, plugging in and downloading.

The other interesting thing was that as soon as I started my meditation with this remedy, I could hear the call to prayer. That was confirmation to me that we are called to receive.

- **Energy Center:** Crown and Transpersonal Point
- **Element:** Metal
- **Meridian:** Lung
- **Number Vibration:** 5 in Spirit
- **Affirmation**: *I hear the Divine's call and I move towards the Source.*

TAMR HENNA HINDI
Lagerstroemia indica
Keynote: Community

Tamr Henna Hindi is a small bushy shrub with dark green leaves. It has very delicate light pink flowers, which form clusters within clusters. The flowers themselves are light pink and ruffled.

This remedy is for connecting groups of people in a very light, loving way, with lots of movement, and childlike play, good for positive family interactions. Satellites revolve around a planet, finding the connection of belonging in a fun, joyful way. Connecting the energies of related individuals (primordial connection or reconnection), it is a very joyful remedy.

- **Energy Center:** Heart
- **Element:** Fire
- **Meridian:** Triple Warmer
- **Number Vibration:** 3 in Matter
- **Affirmation:** *I joyfully connect to those around me.*

The Sacred Sites

DENDERA TEMPLE
Chapel of the Union
Keynote: Sacred Marriage

D endera Temple is a temple in Upper Egypt, north of Luxor. The temple is devoted to Hat-hor—goddess of love and empowerment. She is the mother earth archetype, the Divine Feminine. She represented the *sacred cow*, the second sign of the zodiac before the patriarchy made it a bull, Taurus. Interestingly enough, the remedy was made May 14th, 2004, during her zodiacal month.

Hat-hor is all about vibration. Her instrument is the sistrum. The ancient texts explain how movement is life, creation, and how things that don't move are dead and decay. I see her as the mother of vibration. The goddess animates and creates life.

The remedy was prepared in a very special place in Dendera Temple, The *Chapel of the Union*. The chapel is on the roof of the temple. It was the place of the sacred marriage between Hat-hor and Horus the Elder. This point emanates very strong Hat-hor energy. The holy statue of Hat-hor was potentized at this spot during Pharaonic times. The statue was then used in rituals at the temple, and once a year it was taken on a trip up the Nile to Horus the Elder's temple in Edfu.

Because this is an environmental remedy, it is used to shift the energy of a space, to create a sacred space for transformation or as an elixir in a ritual for invoking Hat-hor or the sacred marriage.

TEMPLE OF THE SUN
Venus transit, June 8, 2004
Keynote: Portal

The Temple of the Sun is located in Giza south of the Great Pyramids in Egypt. It is near the Abusir pyramids. It has an altar made of quartz crystal, the only one known in Egypt. Quartz, as a stone, is for holding information or power.

The altar itself is in the form of the famous mandala of an eight-pointed star, the same mandala that is seen in Angkor Wat in Cambodia. The eight-pointed star signifies Venus/Inanna/Hat-hor/Sirius or the *eight-division sky place* of the Mayans. It is a portal to the galactic center.

In the center of the eight-pointed star is a perfectly cut six-foot circle that is actually a shaft going down more than a hundred feet into the earth. The shaft connects to the ancient waterway that still runs below.

This remedy was made at a very auspicious moment, the important Venus transit on June 8th, 2004. The remedy holds the very strong subtle feminine energy emanated by the planet Venus (Hat-hor), potentized by the Sun during the transit and captured on the altar of the Temple of the Sun. It is a good remedy to aid us in times of great shifts. It works as a portal to the higher dimensions.

Glossary

Chakra is a Sanskrit word meaning "spinning wheel". Chakras are vortices of energy in the body. The chakras system is the most common nomenclature used in healing modalities to express specific energy centers. Each one lies over an endocrine gland, funneling energy into the body and activating the gland. The chakras have correspondences in different senses and aspects such as color, musical note, taste, etc.

Hat-hor was the very ancient Egyptian goddess/*neter* of love, beauty and empowerment. She represents the Divine Feminine, the mother archetype and the sacred cow. With Sekhmet, she comprises the two aspects of the Serpent Goddess. After the Age of Aries, and the onset of patriarchy, she was pushed aside and almost forgotten.

Isis was a lesser goddess. She was a high priestess of Hat-hor. With the rise of the Sun god Ra, the patriarchy, and the separation of the Serpent Goddesses, the brother-sister *netru* rose to prominence.

Koshk is an Arabic word, which means "kiosk", a small wooden building. Houses in Egypt are usually stone or brick, rarely will you find a wooden house and so a wooden house may be referred to as a *koshk*, regardless of its size.

Light Languages are messages of direct communication with Source/Light. There are many explanations as to what light languages are and how they are spoken, communicated and what their purpose is, but ultimately they are *divine* communication. It is well known that DNA (and our whole body) emits light, so light languages can be thought of as a very basic or primordial form of communication. For this reason, we can use waveforms such as light (and sound) to communicate with or activate this light in our bodies and cells.

Meridians are energy channels that run through the body in the Chinese system of medicine. They are used in many modalities such as acupuncture, acupressure and Touch For Health, among many others.

Miasm is a term used to explain a distortion in the energetic blueprint, specifically a distortion that can be passed on generation to generation. The word was coined by Samuel Hahnemann to explain chronic and familial diseases. It originally comes from the Greek *miasma*, which means "stain", or "pollution". In homeopathy, it refers to something such as a disease that has altered, disrupted or "polluted" a healthy energetic pattern. The disrupted energetic pattern is then imprinted on the DNA and passed down through generations until it can be healed and reestablish its healthy pattern. Hahnemann also noted that the individual did not need to actually acquire the disease; fear of the disease would be enough to cause a disruption in the energetic pattern.

Mother Tincture is the first, undiluted remedy preparation. It is the original water that was potentized by the flowers, in the sunlight. This means the dilution is zero. Alcohol is added to the water fraction to preserve the water fraction but it is not considered a dilution unless more water is added.

Muscle testing is a method used in modalities such as Touch For Health. The practitioner tests the client's muscle by asking the client to hold, or resist, their attempt to push down their arm or a designated *strong* muscle. It is almost like a lie-detector test. In *truth* or *integrity*, the client will be able to hold the muscle strong. When there is a disruption, the muscle will not hold.

Nadi is a Sanskrit word. It refers to the subtle energy channels that flow through the body. It is similar to meridians in the Chinese medicine system. All the nadis converge in the navel, making it an incredibly potent center, energetically.

Neter (netru pl.) means archetype or aspect of nature. The word dates back to the Pharaonic times and was mistranslated by Egyptologists to mean "god". The ancient language had no vowels, like many Middle Eastern languages, so the original hieroglyphic characters represented were *ntr*, which when vowels are added, becomes the word "nature" in almost every language.

Number Vibrations (Universal Vibrational Harmonics) is work that was channeled and taught by Rita Hiri. It is a system of numerology, which takes numbers down to their very essence, their archetypal vibration. Rita's work illuminates the essential nature of the remedies by aligning them with the number vibrations or Universal Vibrational Harmonics. By using different calculation, we can determine the number vibration of a cycle and use a remedy accordingly.

Potentization is the act of imprinting a matrix or giving "potential" to a substance. It comes from the Latin *potentia* meaning "power". When the mother tincture is then further diluted and succussed repeatedly, the energy of a substance can be driven-up. This is a process used in the preparation of homeopathic remedies, which is why they are found in different *potencies* (6X, 200C, 1M, etc.). The power of a substance is increased through a progressive process of dilution and succussion.

Samuel Hahnemann was a late 18th century physician who was considered "the father of homeopathy". He was a visionary working in a time long before energetic healing or even DNA had been acknowledged. His most famous work *Organon of the Medical Art* is considered by many to be one of the most comprehensive books not only on homeopathy but also on health, disease and medical care.

Shadow Work was a phrase coined by the Swiss psychologist Carl Jung. The theory is that all the denied or unwanted aspects of ourselves are put into the *shadow* so as not to be seen or dealt with. There are many reasons for this, but the point to note is that even though we are usually not conscious of what these aspects are, they still take energy from us. Shadow work is the process of unraveling the mystery of what is in the shadow, usually with a therapist, and re-incorporating those aspects back into our consciousness so that the issues can be dealt with in the light and will no longer drain our energy.

Succussion is a vigorous shaking or strong movement with impact. It is the method by which homeopathic remedies are potentized. In a closed vessel, the energy present in a substance is driven up by repeated impact. If a container is open, strong impact will discharge the energy (such as running water purifying itself) but in a closed system the energy folds back on itself and is increased.

Touch For Health (TFH) is a system of kinesiology developed by John F. Thie, DC in the 1970s. The system is based on the fact that all major muscles in the body eventually connect to a meridian (Chinese system of energy channels) in the body.

By testing specific muscles we can determine which meridians are weak and which are over-working. The body can then be balanced using several techniques.

Vibration/frequency is the most basic component of the universe. It is energy, waves. Everything that lives or is *animated* vibrates and has a frequency.

Bibliography

Hahnemann, Samuel, and Wenda Brewster Reilly. *Organon of the Medical Art*. Redmond, Wash.: Birdcage Books, 1996.

> Samuel Hahnemann's work on *miasms* as well as his work on energy medicine in general is an important resource when working with any type of remedies. Although this is not an easy book to read, it is recommended for any practitioner working with energetic substances.

McGarey, William A. *The Oil That Heals: A Physician's Successes with Castor Oil Treatments*. Virginia Beach, Va.: A.R.E. Press, 1993.

> This book is about Edgar Cayce's work with castor oil—known as the *Palm of Christ*. Cayce recommended it for a huge range of ailments. In the book the author alludes to the fact that Cayce believed it was more the energy of the plant rather than the extracted oil, that contained the healing power, which would explain why it could be used for such a great number of conditions. Had flower remedies been more commonly used at that point in time, he might have used the remedy rather than the oil.

Resources

Al-chemia and Egyptian Flower Remedies Website:
http://www.egyptianflowerremedies.com

I briefly mentioned Felicitas Goodman's important work. She was an anthropologist who presented the idea of *Ecstatic Trance Postures*. Her work is worth looking at by anyone interested in ecstatic states or wishing to do inter-dimensional work. The Cuyamungue Institute was started by her and has continued on with her work even after she crossed over. For more information on their activities, go to their website:
http://www.cuyamungueinstitute.com

Ian Lungold was an artist with a passion for the Mayan Calendar. He worked with Carl Calleman at the end of his life. During his time on Earth, he presented many talks and videos about the Mayan calendar from a more artistic, easy to understand, point of view. To watch his videos or listen to interviews, see the Mayan Majix website or his interviews on sites such as Red Ice Creations:
http://www.mayanmajix.com/ian.html

Rita Hiri's original work is Vibration Numerology. She can be found in many places on the web, search for her by her name, Vibrational Numerology or Shaping Energy.

Touch For Health is one of the modalities we used in our research with the Al-chemia Remedies. There are many TFH websites and practitioners. To find out more, you can do a search for Touch For Health, John F. Thie or his son Matthew Thie.

Dr. Masuru Emoto and Jacques Benveniste were both pioneers in the field of potentization, showing how substances can imprint on water. Their groundbreaking work is a must for any student of flower or homeopathic remedies. Dr. Emoto has many books and DVD's on his work. Search for him by his name, or his work "Messages from Water". To learn more about Jacques Benveniste search for Michel Schiff who has written a book about Benveniste's life and persecution by mainstream science.

Schiff, Michel. *The Memory of Water: Homoeopathy and the Battle of Ideas in the New Science.* London: Thorsons, 1995.

Anodea Judith is one of the best-known writers in the West in the field of chakra work. She has many excellent books for working with the chakras. My favorite is the following book, which gives overviews and tables of the correspondences as well as information about the emotional issues related to the chakras:

Judith, Anodea. *Eastern Body, Western Mind: Psychology and the Chakra System as a Path to the Self.* Berkeley, Calif.: Celestial Arts, 1996.

Printed in the United States
By Bookmasters